Many dogs like to swim.

There's even one kind of swimming named for dogs. It's called the dog paddle!

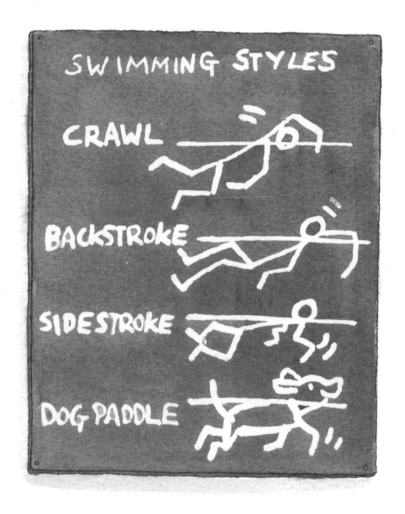

When boys and girls learn
to swim, they often start by
doing the dog paddle.

You can watch how a dog
swims. Then a teacher can
show you how to swim.

First, jump into a pond. Keep your head out of the water.

Keep your arms underwater.
Paddle them back and forth.
Kick and splash with your legs.

If you want to be silly, you
can even fetch a ball or a stick!

When you get out of the
water, shake yourself off.

Then wag your tail and bark
with glee!